Encoded in Stone:
The Memory of Earth & the
Story of Us

Encoded in Stone: The Memory of Earth and the Story of Us
© 2025 Gia Snyder
All rights reserved.

Published by Rooted Hound Press
www.rootedhoundpress.com
Edited and produced in the United States of America.

ISBN: 978-1-969687-10-5

Printed in the United States of America.
10 9 8 7 6 5 4 3 2 1

Table of Contents

Author's Introduction..v

Preface vii

A Note on Perspective...ix

Prologue: **What the Earth Remembers** xi

CHAPTER ONE — The Call of the Stone 1

CHAPTER TWO — **The Spiral Within the Earth** 6

CHAPTER THREE — **Sacred Sites as Star Maps**........................11

CHAPTER FOUR — **Builders of Light and Stone**........................17

CHAPTER FIVE — **When the Stones Speak**...............................22

CHAPTER SIX — **Hidden in Plain Sight**...................................28

CHAPTER SEVEN — **Warnings from the Ancients** 34

CHAPTER EIGHT — **Gateways and Guardians** 40

CHAPTER NINE — **The Awakening Grid**...................................46

CHAPTER TEN — **Buried Memory and Living Stone**..................52

CHAPTER ELEVEN — **The Sound of Stone**................................58

CHAPTER TWELVE — **Encoded in Stone** 64

CHAPTER THIRTEEN — **The Stone Within** 69

CHAPTER FOURTEEN — **The Conversation Continues** 74

CHAPTER FIFTEEN — **Memory In The Landscape: The Earth as an Active Participant**...78

CHAPTER SIXTEEN — **The Continuity of Human Ingenuity**.......84

CONCLUSION — **What The Stones Remember** 90

Epilogue — **The Memory We Carry Forward**............................95

For the Earth,
who remembers everything we forget.

Author's Introduction

This book is part of a larger body of work exploring the journey of human consciousness across multiple levels: the inner world, the cosmic world, and the world beneath our feet.

Book One explored the inner landscape of the soul — personal healing, identity, and the return to wholeness.

Book Two expanded outward, examining consciousness within a larger cosmic framework: patterns, symbols, synchronicities, and the larger forces that shape personal awakening.

This book, Book Three, focuses on the physical context in which all of that unfolds. It examines the Earth itself — not as metaphor, but as evidence. As a record of cycles, environmental shifts, cultural resets, and the structures that humanity built to withstand them.

Together, these three books form a progression:

Book One: the *soul*

Book Two: the *cosmos*

Book Three: the *Earth-body memory*

This book serves as the grounding point, connecting the internal and the cosmic to the historical and geological. It situates spiritual awakening within the broader timeline of the planet, showing what humanity has survived, adapted to, and remembered through the material record.

While the previous volumes addressed symbolic and spiritual interpretation, **this volume addresses the physical evidence** — what is known, what is uncertain, and what the Earth preserves when written history is absent.

It is not a conclusion but a foundation — the bridge between personal evolution and the long arc of human history.

Preface

My work has always moved between two worlds. One is the inner world—the place of intuition, memory, and quiet truth that rises from within. The other is the physical world—the measurable, observable reality shaped by the Earth itself. These two ways of understanding life are not in conflict; they complement one another. The spiritual and the material reflect different dimensions of the same human experience.

As I wrote the first two books of this series, I explored the soul and the larger cosmic framework in which we exist. Those books speak to the internal and the infinite. This book turns toward the ground beneath our feet. It is a reminder that the Earth also holds memory, and that the physical structures left behind by ancient people reveal a story of resilience, ingenuity, and adaptation.

While my personal worldview includes spiritual ideas that extend beyond what archaeology can measure, I have kept this volume firmly grounded in evidence. The ancient world deserves to be understood through what can be known, not through assumptions or speculation. Yet it is equally true that the reason I was drawn to this subject at all is because I feel deeply connected to the Earth—to its cycles, its upheavals, its quiet shifts, and the sense of remembrance embedded in its landscapes.

This book does not attempt to resolve the mysteries of early civilizations or reinterpret them through spiritual frameworks. It presents what the stones can support. But my broader journey, and the larger series this book belongs to, is shaped by the belief that physical history, inner experience, and spiritual insight all contribute to our understanding of who we are.

This is the bridge between them.

— *Gia*

A Note on Perspective

This book approaches ancient architecture and early societies from a strictly evidence-based standpoint. My intention is to offer a clear and grounded interpretation of what the archaeological and geological records can reliably support.

At the same time, I recognize that many readers, like myself, hold spiritual understandings that extend beyond the limits of measurable data. My own worldview includes spiritual concepts that do not appear in this volume—not because they are unimportant, but because they fall outside the scope of material evidence.

This book is one part of a larger body of work. Other volumes in this series explore intuition, consciousness, symbolism, and the inner dimension of human experience. This one is dedicated to the physical record: what the Earth preserves, what the stones reveal, and what science can confidently reconstruct.

Multiple ways of knowing can exist side by side. This book represents one of them.

Prologue: What the Earth Remembers

The Earth carries a longer memory than humanity does. Civilizations emerge, expand, adapt, and disappear. Climate shifts. Sea levels rise and fall. Volcanoes alter landscapes in a single day. Ice advances, retreats, and erases what once stood in its path. Across these cycles, only a few forms of human expression survive—and stone is one of them.

Stone does not preserve everything. It does not record names, languages, or daily life in complete detail. But it holds structural choices, alignments, tool marks, and intentional patterns that outlast every other material. When the written record is limited or absent, stone becomes the primary evidence of how people lived, what they valued, and how they understood their world.

This book is not about speculation or myth. It is an examination of what the Earth itself makes available through geology, archaeology, and the physical remnants of ancient cultures. It is about what can be verified, what can be reasonably interpreted, and what remains unknown.

Humanity has lived through environmental shifts and periods of instability before. Archaeology and geology together show clear cycles of climate change, population disruption, and cultural rebuilding. In these transitions, written memory often disappears. Oral history breaks. Technology regresses. Entire traditions fade within a few generations.

What remains, when everything else is gone, are the structures built deliberately to endure. Temples. Monoliths. Stone circles. Foundations aligned to the sky. Carved walls that survived fire, water, and time. These structures are not simply architectural achievements; they are data. They record human capacity, knowledge, and intention at moments far earlier than modern timelines once assumed.

To study them is to study the long arc of human adaptation—how societies responded to environmental pressure, how they reestablished order after disruption, and how they preserved meaning when stability returned. This book follows that arc. It traces the evidence left in stone, examines what the Earth records during periods of sudden change, considers how memory is preserved across ages without relying on written documents, and explores the repeated patterns that appear independently across early human cultures.

We are living in a time when interest in the ancient world is increasing, not because of fantasy or escapism, but because the patterns of the past are becoming relevant again. Environmental volatility forces us to look not only forward but backward—toward the societies that faced similar challenges and left behind the physical evidence of how they responded.

Stone endures. It preserves decisions, alignments, and adaptations from people who lived through earlier turning points in human history. Understanding what they left behind is not about rewriting the past. It is about understanding the continuity of human resilience. This is the purpose of *Encoded in Stone*: to examine what the Earth remembers, and to consider what it means for us now.

CHAPTER ONE — The Call of the Stone

There is a whisper that lives in stone. Not a sound, not a voice, but a presence — something that moves through mountains, temples, megaliths, and broken ruins the same way breath moves through a body. It doesn't travel through the air but through your bones. You don't hear it with your ears. You feel it. A magnetic pull. A vibration beneath the skin. A memory your soul recognizes long before your mind catches up.

Some people call it curiosity. Others call it wanderlust. But those who feel it know better. It's a calling.

Why does the sight of moss-covered stones or the stillness of an ancient temple stir something so deep within us? Why do some locations — places we've never been in this life — feel familiar, comforting, or haunting? Why do our eyes well up when we stand among ruins? Why does our breath catch when we place our hand on a weathered stone that has seen centuries rise and fall?

1

Because stone is more than material. Stone is memory made manifest.

Throughout human history, people have traveled to sacred places not just to pray, bury their dead, or honor the gods — but to remember. These sites were built on purpose, on power points where the Earth's breath rises more clearly, where the veil thins, and where time feels soft. Our ancestors understood something we are only beginning to rediscover: that the Earth is alive, conscious, and encoded with wisdom. And where the land speaks strongest, stone becomes its language.

Standing stones, pyramids, temples, dolmens, stone circles, passage graves — these were not placed randomly. They were built where Earth energy braids upward, where ley lines cross, where magnetic fields shift, or where ancient starlight once mirrored the ground. These places act like crystalline transmitters — not metaphorically, but literally. Granite, quartz, basalt, and limestone all carry piezoelectric properties. When pressure or sound moves through them, they respond.

Some sites hum. Some amplify intention. Some alter states of consciousness. Some awaken memory.

When we say sacred sites "call" to us, we are speaking both poetically and physically. The stones are transmitting — resonating with the frequency of consciousness, emotion, and Earth energy. And those who are sensitive feel the signal.

To be called to the stones is to be called back to yourself.

For the temples of the ancient world were not passive structures. They were built as tuning forks — resonators crafted from stone, geometry, and star alignment to awaken something dormant within the human soul. Their builders knew that memory isn't stored only in the mind. It is stored in energy. In place. In vibration. In stone.

This is why a sacred site doesn't need to be intact to hold its power. Even broken stones remember. Even ruins pulse. Even a single fallen block from a long-destroyed temple can still feel alive, carrying centuries of intention, offerings, ceremony, and encoded wisdom.

You can feel it when you walk among them — that shift in the air, the quiet awareness, the sense that something is both watching you and welcoming you.

Some say these are echoes of the past. Others say they're remnants of forgotten civilizations. But perhaps they are neither. Perhaps they are invitations.

> Invitations to listen.
> To feel.
> To remember.

Because the more you tune into these places, the more something begins to stir — not around you, but within you. A remembering that you, too, are made of Earth. That your bones carry the same minerals as the stones. That the Earth's memory lives in you as well.

These places don't teach in words. They teach in resonance — through the way your body reacts, through intuitive knowing, through the quiet pull toward the deeper truth.

The stones speak. And if you're holding this book, you've already begun to hear them.

This chapter is not an introduction to ancient sites. It is an initiation into remembering.

As we continue through these pages, we will journey through spirals, star maps, lost civilizations, portals, and the energetic architecture beneath the Earth itself. These are not stories of people long gone. They are stories of consciousness — stories written into stone for those who would one day return to read them. Not with their eyes. But with their soul.

Because what is encoded in stone is also encoded in you.

CHAPTER TWO — The Spiral Within the Earth

There is a pattern woven through the world — older than language, older than symbols, older even than memory. It appears in the swirl of galaxies, the curl of ocean waves, the unfurling of ferns, the shape of hurricanes, and the double helix of DNA. The ancients carved it into stone, painted it on cave walls, shaped it into pottery, and built it into the layout of their sacred sites. The spiral is not just art. It is a map.

The spiral shows us how energy moves. Not in straight lines, but in loops and curves, returning again and again to the same point from a higher, expanded vantage. Evolution is not a ladder. It is a spiral staircase rising through time. Healing does not occur in a single moment. It spirals through layers. Consciousness does not advance linearly. It expands in cycles — outward and inward, above and below — the same way the Earth breathes through seasons, tides, and magnetic shifts.

We were not merely observers of this pattern. We were participants in it.

Ancient peoples saw the spiral in the sky and recognized it in their own consciousness. They mirrored it in labyrinths, sacred carvings, temple layouts, and sun-wheel symbols. The spiral was used to teach the initiatory path: the journey from the outer world of form into the inner world of truth. To walk the spiral, whether drawn in sand or carved into stone, was to enact the journey of awakening.

This pattern is embedded not only in symbolism and art, but in the Earth herself.

Across the planet are locations where energy seems to rise, twist, or converge — where the land carries a charge that awakens something in those who visit. These vortexes often follow spiral flows of magnetic and telluric energy, creating pockets where thought becomes clearer, emotion intensifies, intuition sharpens, or time feels strange. Sedona, Glastonbury, Uluru, Mount Shasta — each is known not only for its beauty but for its energetic spiral.

These places were not chosen randomly. The ancients recognized where the Earth's energy gathered, where the spiral currents converged, and built structures that reflected and amplified those flows. Stone circles, stepped pyramids, terraced mountainsides, and concentric temples often mimic spiral geometry — not as decoration, but as resonance.

Even pilgrimage paths echo the spiral. A seeker walks in circles, slowly narrowing toward a sacred center. With each turn, the outer world falls away, and the inner world grows louder. The spiral becomes a teacher, guiding the traveler into deeper presence, deeper truth, deeper remembrance.

The Earth's spiral isn't symbolic. It is literal — a natural law of energy. Geomagnetic currents spiral around the planet in flowing lines. Water spirals as it moves through rivers and underground aquifers. Atmospheric patterns spiral in storms and winds. Even the Earth's molten core generates spiraling magnetic fields that interact with our own electromagnetic bodies.

When ancient builders aligned their temples with spirals in the land, they were not following superstition. They were harmonizing with the planet's energetic anatomy.

This relationship between Earth and sky is reflected in architecture as well. Some of the world's most enigmatic structures embody spiral geometry in their design. At Chichen

Itza, the ancient Maya built El Caracol — "the snail" — an observatory with a spiral staircase aligned to celestial events. Stone circles like those in Scotland and Ireland contain concentric rings radiating outward like ripples in water. Even the Great Pyramid contains subtle spiral proportions hidden within its dimensions — a geometric signature linking Earth, sky, and consciousness.

Across cultures, the spiral was a reminder: we are not separate from the universe's pattern. We are shaped by it. We move with it. We awaken through it.

To follow the spiral is to follow the path of consciousness itself — returning again and again to places we thought we understood, only to see them from a new angle, a higher point on the curve. Each return is not repetition. It is expansion.

And perhaps that is why the spiral calls to us still. It speaks the language of the soul — a language we do not learn, but remember. A language that reminds us where we come from, where we are going, and what has always been moving within us.

The spiral is the universe in motion. The Earth in motion. Our consciousness in motion. And as we shift into a time of remembering, the spiral becomes not just a pattern — but a guide.

It invites us inward. It invites us upward. It invites us home.

CHAPTER THREE — Sacred Sites as Star Maps

Long before maps were drawn on parchment, the sky itself was the map — a living record of cycles, stories, and celestial pathways. Ancient cultures didn't simply observe the stars; they studied them, honored them, and mirrored them on Earth. To align with the heavens was to align with divine order. To build in harmony with the stars was to remember where we came from.

Across continents and millennia, sacred sites reveal a stunning truth: many of the world's most important structures were designed as reflections of the sky above them. Not symbolically, but with astonishing precision.

Perhaps no site is more iconic than the Giza Plateau. The three pyramids — Khufu, Khafre, and Menkaure — are arranged to mirror the three stars of Orion's Belt: Alnitak, Alnilam, and Mintaka. The alignment is not approximate; it is deliberate, echoing the size, spacing, and offset of the stars with architectural accuracy. In ancient Egypt, Orion was associated with Osiris, the god of resurrection. To mirror that constellation in stone was to anchor the soul's journey into physical form. The pyramids were not tombs. They were star temples.

The deeper we look, the more layers we uncover. Shafts within the Great Pyramid point directly toward Sirius and Orion — not as air ducts, but as celestial alignments. Modern muon scans have revealed hidden chambers above the Grand Gallery, suggesting harmonics, resonance, or encoded knowledge still sealed within. Every aspect of the Great Pyramid — its angle, its dimensions, its placement — embeds mathematical relationships tied to Earth's size, curvature, and even precessional cycles. In stone, the builders carved a map of the cosmos.

But Giza is not an isolated phenomenon. Across the world, we see the same pattern: sacred structures placed with intention, aligned to solstices, equinoxes, star clusters, and planetary movements.

At Stonehenge, massive stones frame the rising sun on the summer solstice with such precision that light travels directly through the ancient archway. At Chaco Canyon in New Mexico, ceremonial buildings track lunar standstill cycles — a phenomenon so rare and complex it requires an 18.6-year observation period. At Machu Picchu, the Intihuatana stone casts shadows that mark solar cycles and seasonal changes with exacting detail. In Cambodia, Angkor Wat mirrors the constellation Draco at the time of its construction, encoding celestial myth into temple geometry. In Mexico, the pyramids of Teotihuacan align with the Pleiades, as if the city was designed as a cosmic diagram.

Even older still is the site of Nabta Playa in southern Egypt, where stone circles predating Stonehenge by thousands of years map the rising of Orion and Sirius. These early sky-watchers aligned megaliths with celestial events that marked seasonal cycles, migration patterns, and spiritual stories written in the heavens.

Why this global obsession with the stars?

Because to ancient cultures, the sky was not separate from Earth — it was a mirror. A teacher. A reminder of origins. Many believed that humanity itself was seeded from star realms and that aligning with certain constellations created harmony between the physical and spiritual worlds. Sacred sites became cosmic anchors, bringing the heavens down to Earth through stone, geometry, and ceremony.

These alignments also served practical and prophetic functions. By tracking the sky, ancient people could foresee seasonal changes, time agricultural cycles, predict solar and lunar events, and mark the turning of great ages. Some structures encode precession — the slow wobble of Earth's axis — across spans of thousands of years, suggesting a level of astronomical knowledge far beyond what mainstream history typically credits.

But perhaps the deeper purpose was remembrance.

The builders of these star-aligned temples seemed to understand that human consciousness is influenced not only by Earthly energy but by cosmic rhythm. As planets align, as stars rise and set, as the heavens move across their cycles, something within us responds. We feel it in our dreams, in our intuition, in the quiet pull toward certain places or questions. The ancients listened to this pull. They saw the stars not as distant lights but as beacons — markers of destiny, memory, and cosmic identity.

When we walk through a sacred site aligned to the heavens, we are stepping into a conversation between Earth and sky. The stones guide our eyes upward. The alignments guide our awareness inward. We remember the vastness of our origin and the precision with which our ancestors wove that origin into matter.

These ancient builders were not decorating landscapes. They were encoding cosmology. They were marking the relationship between humanity and the universe, carving into stone what the soul already knows: we are part of something celestial, something cyclical, something far older than any written history.

When we stand at these star-aligned sites today — whether at dawn in Giza, at dusk in Chaco Canyon, or beneath a solstice sun at Stonehenge — something stirs. Not in the stones, but in us. A subtle recognition. A hum beneath the ribs. A whisper rising from memory.

> Look up, the stones say.
> Look within, the sky echoes back.

Sacred sites remind us that Earth is not separate from the cosmos. She is part of it — a node in a greater celestial web. And each alignment carved into stone invites us to remember that we, too, are part of that web. Not by belief, but by resonance.

The ground we walk upon may be more than history. It may be a mirror of home.

CHAPTER FOUR — Builders of Light and Stone

We marvel at the monuments they left behind — the pyramids aligned to the stars, the stone circles tuned to the sun, the temples carved with impossible precision. Yet for all our admiration, we know surprisingly little about the people who built them. Mainstream history tells a simple story: early civilizations, primitive tools, long labor, and ingenuity. But when you stand before these ancient structures, when you feel the precision, the resonance, the planetary alignment, something deeper stirs.

Something in us knows this was not simple.

These builders were not just stacking stones. They were shaping consciousness.

Across traditions and continents, whispers remain of earlier cultures — civilizations that rose, fell, and left behind fragments of profound knowledge. In the West, this memory appears as Atlantis: a society said to possess advanced understanding of geometry, astronomy, and energy. In the East and Pacific, the parallel is Lemuria or Mu — a heart-centered civilization in harmony with the Earth and the crystalline matrix beneath her surface.

Modern scholars dismiss these stories as myth, but myth is often a language of memory — not literal, but encoded truth. A way for ancient peoples to preserve what could not be spoken outright. A way to carry forward knowledge of rises and falls, of golden ages and great catastrophes, of wisdom saved through initiates and symbols.

Whoever these early cultures were, their influence echoes in the architecture that followed. The builders of the megalithic world were more than engineers — they were initiates working with sacred geometry, celestial timing, resonance, and stone as a living medium. Their monuments reflect an understanding of Earth not as inert land, but as a conscious being with energy lines, magnetic flows, and harmonic points.

These were builders who knew the Earth's grid — who sensed where energy rose, where the veil thinned, where communication with higher realms was possible. They placed their structures on these nodal points with intention, creating temples that functioned not only as ceremonial centers, but as vibrational instruments. Through sound, alignment, and geometry, they tuned human consciousness to the Earth and the cosmos.

Such knowledge does not arise from simple observation alone. It is inherited. Remembered. Carried. The idea that these builders were students of a deeper lineage is woven throughout ancient myth: stories of "sky people," "shining ones," "serpent teachers," or wisdom bringers who came "from the stars" to guide early humanity. Whether literal or symbolic, the message is the same: the knowledge was not born randomly. It descended.

Over time, as cycles turned and civilizations rose and fell, much of this knowledge faded from the everyday world. But it did not disappear. It moved underground — into mystery schools, into priesthoods, into encoded symbols, into stone itself. The great temples of Egypt, the pyramids of Mesoamerica, the megalithic circles of Europe, the monoliths of the Andes — all carry remnants of this inheritance.

These people were not building to worship. They were building to transmit.

The structures they created served multiple layers of purpose. A pyramid could be a tomb, a temple, a calendar, a resonance chamber, and a cosmic mirror all at once. A stone circle could track the solstice, anchor the Earth's energy at a nodal point, and serve as a ceremonial gateway for spiritual initiation. A labyrinth wasn't just a design — it was a map of consciousness.

The builders understood that matter responds to intention. That geometry shapes energy. That vibration influences awareness. They worked with stone the way modern scientists work with frequency — deliberately, precisely, with a long view of time.

When we stand before these ancient structures today, we feel something because they were built to make us feel. Their purpose was not only to serve the people of their own era but to speak across ages. To hold memory through cycles of forgetting. To awaken something in those who would return thousands of years later — a message carved in matter, waiting for consciousness to rise enough to hear it again.

These echoes of ancient wisdom are not fantasy. They are recognition. We feel them because something within us remembers. The same spiral that moves through the stars moves through our DNA. The same geometry embedded in temples lives in our bodies. The same resonance carved into stone resonates in our bones.

Perhaps this is the greatest legacy of these builders: not the monuments themselves, but the remembrance they trigger. Each stone, each alignment, each carved symbol is a reminder of a relationship humanity once had with the Earth — a partnership based on harmony, reverence, and awareness of the unseen.

We are not just studying ancient builders. We are reawakening the part of ourselves that understands why they built the way they did. A part that knows Earth is alive. A part that knows consciousness is shaped through place. A part that knows the stars are not distant — they are home.

The deeper we look at these structures, the more the old explanations fall away. These were not primitive engineers. They were builders of light and stone — architects of memory, keepers of frequency, and stewards of a wisdom that still lives, quietly, beneath the surface of our world.

And now, as cycles turn once more, that wisdom is rising again.

CHAPTER FIVE — When the Stones Speak

There is a reason people travel thousands of miles just to stand among ancient stones. It's not simply curiosity or tourism. It's something felt — a pull, a hum, a subtle shift that seems to rise from the ground and move through the body. Some places feel awake. Some feel watchful. Some feel as though they've been waiting.

Many sacred sites are not silent relics but living structures, still interacting with the Earth's energetic field and with anyone who steps into their presence. They rest on ley lines, geomagnetic anomalies, and natural vortex points where the Earth's energy rises and spirals. The ancients built on these places deliberately, aligning their structures not only with the heavens but with the energetic pulse of the land beneath their feet.

When you enter these spaces, something in the atmosphere changes. Your breath shifts. Your awareness sharpens. The boundary between the physical and the subtle becomes thin.

You feel the memory held by the stone — not as a story, but as a resonance.

Visitors describe a wide range of sensations: tingling in the palms or feet, warmth moving up the spine, sudden emotional release, a drop into stillness, or a feeling of being gently observed. Time can stretch or soften. Thoughts become quieter. Intuition becomes clearer. It's as if the site is tuning you — the way a musician tunes an instrument before playing.

This is not imagination. Many of these effects can be measured. Magnetometers spike. Compasses misalign. EMF meters flicker or go silent. In some places, sound behaves strangely — echoing, bending, or disappearing entirely. In others, electronics glitch or refuse to operate. The land is active. The stones respond.

At Sedona, people often speak of being drawn to certain rock formations without knowing why, only to find themselves flooded with emotion or clarity. At Machu Picchu, many describe feeling as though they're walking through a dream — the air thick with silence, the mountains holding something ancient and alive. Inside the Great Pyramid, a single hum can vibrate through the entire chamber, carrying through the bones in a way that defies explanation. At Stonehenge and Avebury, compasses can spin, and sensitive visitors report a buzzing underfoot, as if the ground is softly electrified.

These sites are not static. They are participants.

The ancients understood that stone has memory — not metaphorically, but literally. Quartz and granite, common in many sacred sites, possess piezoelectric properties. Sound, pressure, and energy cause them to vibrate and respond. When arranged with intention, they become instruments — tuned to Earth's frequency, aligned with celestial cycles, and responsive to human presence.

When we say the stones "speak," we are not talking about words. We are talking about resonance. About the subtle way a place can meet you, reflect you, or awaken something within you. It may arrive as a sudden emotion. A sensation. A knowing. A "yes" rising from the quiet center of your being.

Some people feel called to certain sites without understanding why — only to stand there and feel a sense of recognition so deep it brings tears. Others feel gently pushed away from places that are not meant for them, as if the land itself whispers,

"Not today." These experiences are real. These places have presence. And that presence responds to intention, respect, and alignment.

I've felt these shifts myself.

During an investigation at Gettysburg — a place heavy with emotional and energetic residue — I sensed a presence across the road from where our group stood. I couldn't see a figure clearly, but I knew it was there. My entire body responded: a wave of dizziness, an inner push to step back, a sense of crossing an invisible threshold. When I walked off the bridge, the feeling lifted instantly. When I returned, it slammed back into me. That wasn't fear. It wasn't imagination. It was the land speaking — through energy, through memory, through a boundary I could feel but not see.

Not every site needs technology to tell its story. Some speak directly to the body.

The Earth is alive. She has meridians, nodes, and chakras — energetic centers that have pulsed for millennia. Sacred sites built on these nodes act like amplifiers, gateways, or thresholds where the veil between worlds thins. They can offer healing, clarity, initiation, or remembrance. They can also protect themselves.

This is why approaching sacred places with reverence matters. These sites respond to intention the way a tuning fork responds to vibration. If you arrive open and grounded, they may meet you. If you arrive disrespectful or demanding, they may shield themselves, or even push back.

The ancients honored these spaces through ritual — not out of superstition, but out of relationship. They understood that when you enter a sacred site, you are entering a living field of memory, intelligence, and presence.

And the presence is not passive.

When stones speak, they speak through sensation, resonance, intuition, and inner knowing. Through the shift in your breath, the stillness in your mind, the tingling beneath your skin. Through the quiet invitation to step inward. These sites were designed to awaken a memory within the human soul — a remembrance of connection, of Earth, of cosmos, of something older than history.

The stones were not placed to mark the past.

They were placed to awaken the future.

To stand among them is to stand in a conversation that began long before you arrived — and continues long after you leave.

CHAPTER SIX — Hidden in Plain Sight

Sacred sites did not disappear when civilizations fell. Many of them simply changed shape. Temples became foundations for churches. Stone circles became grazing fields. Ancient ceremonial grounds became public squares, government buildings, and city centers. The layers of history stack like sediment — each new era building upon the energy of the one before it. But the land remembers. And the geometry remains.

Across the world, structures of modern power sit directly on top of ancient spiritual sites. This is not coincidence. It is continuity. Builders throughout history have recognized the importance of energetic nodes — places where the Earth's magnetic field shifts, where telluric currents rise, where ley lines intersect. These locations carry influence, resonance, and a subtle authority. To build on them is to tap into that power.

In Rome, Christian basilicas were built over pagan temples, which were themselves built over older Etruscan ceremonial sites. Each layer claimed the energy of the one beneath it. In Paris, the Cathedral of Notre-Dame stands on an island that once held a Roman temple dedicated to Jupiter. Beneath the cathedral's foundations, remnants of older structures still hum with the memory of worship, ritual, and alignment. In England, many medieval churches were constructed directly atop stone circles or ancient sacred hills, preserving the energetic potency even as the spiritual narrative changed.

In Washington, D.C., the city's layout reflects principles of sacred geometry, solar alignments, and Masonic symbolism. L'Enfant's street plan forms geometric patterns that echo older European city designs rooted in esoteric knowledge. Obelisks, domes, and compass-oriented axes dot the landscape — not merely as architectural choices, but as energetic markers. The Washington Monument acts as a modern obelisk, mirroring ancient practices in Egypt and Rome where such structures served as anchors of solar energy and political authority.

Many cities follow hidden grid patterns: lines radiating from central monuments, circular roads encircling power centers, and ceremonial avenues aligned to solstices or equinoxes. These designs are not accidental. They reflect an understanding, old and enduring, that geometry shapes consciousness. When a city is built around sacred proportions, it influences the way people move, gather, and think. Geometry is not just mathematics. It is subtle influence.

But not all modern structures maintain the original intention of the land. Sacred geometry can uplift, harmonize, and clarify — but it can also be distorted. When original alignments are altered, when structures are placed without reverence, or when the geometry is inverted, the energy of a place can feel heavy, chaotic, or drained. The land will continue to pulse, but the flow is interrupted.

Some sacred sites were intentionally obscured. Menhirs buried. Dolmens collapsed. Temples dismantled. As Christianity, Islam, and other expanding religions sought to unify belief systems, older practices were suppressed — not only spiritually, but architecturally. Yet even when stones were removed or replaced, the land underneath remained charged. You can still feel the energy at many church altars, even if the original stone circle is long gone. You can still sense the hum beneath city plazas where ancient rituals once took place.

These places hold memory the way the human body holds emotion. Nothing is erased — only transformed.

In some cases, the builders of later eras understood this deeply. Cathedrals rise where ancient worship once took place not to erase the past, but to harness it. Their stained glass, vaulted ceilings, rose windows, and labyrinths echo the geometry of Egyptian temples, megalithic circles, and cosmic diagrams. The symbol changes, the language changes, but the underlying architecture of energy remains.

In other cases, the shift in purpose is more complicated. Power centers — governmental, religious, or institutional — often cluster where ancient structures once stood. The placement is not random. Throughout history, leaders sought locations where the Earth's energy could amplify authority, visibility, and influence. A capital built on a ley line feels different from one built in a neutral field. A courthouse placed on a former temple site carries the resonance of judgment, order, and ritual.

This blending of old and new creates a layered world. A cityscape that is both modern and ancient. A landscape where forgotten temples still pulse beneath pavement. Energetic crossroads hidden beneath parking lots. Ley lines flowing under glass skyscrapers.

When you walk through these places with awareness, you can feel the ancient heartbeat beneath the noise. You may sense a subtle shift in pressure near a government building or cathedral. You may feel a familiar stillness in a public square that once held a stone circle. You may find yourself inexplicably drawn to certain corners, viewpoints, or pathways — pulled by a memory your body recognizes even if your mind does not.

This is the mystery of sacred geography: it never disappears. It adapts.

The Earth's energy grid is older than any civilization, older than any temple, older than any religion. It pulses regardless of what rises above it. Builders who understood this worked with the land. Those who did not still found themselves influenced by it, knowingly or unknowingly.

This chapter is not about hidden conspiracies or secret societies. It is about continuity — the way humanity has always been drawn to the same energetic nodes. The way power, intention, and architecture merge across ages. The way the sacred is never truly lost, only layered.

To see what lies beneath the modern world is not to look backward. It is to remember the foundation — the original design, the original resonance, the original purpose. The ancient grid remains alive, waiting for those who know how to feel beneath the surface.

And once you recognize these layers, the world changes. Cities look different. Churches feel different. Public squares hum with unseen stories. You begin to notice the old geometry shining through the new. You begin to sense the pulse of the Earth beneath brick and asphalt.

You realize that the sacred is not gone.

It is hidden in plain sight.

CHAPTER SEVEN — Warnings from the Ancients

Throughout history, myths and legends have carried echoes of something older than memory — stories of floods, fires, darkness, and rebirth. They appear across continents, separated by language, geography, and time, yet they speak the same language: the world has ended before, and it will change again. These tales were not meant only as stories. They were records. Warnings. Reminders.

Nearly every ancient culture preserves a flood myth. The Sumerian tale of Ziusudra. The Babylonian story of Utnapishtim. The Hebrew account of Noah. The Greek legend of Deucalion. The Maya stories of previous creations washed away. Even Indigenous tribes across the Americas speak of great waters rising, of survivors climbing mountains to escape destruction. These stories share striking details: sudden catastrophe, a world-cleansing event, and a handful of people carrying knowledge into the next age.

But the warnings were not only about water. Many cultures describe ages ending in fire — solar storms, celestial events, or cosmic discharges that reshaped the sky. The Norse spoke of Ragnarok, a cycle of burning and freezing that ends one world and begins another. Hindu cosmology describes yugas, long cycles of rise and decline, punctuated by destruction and renewal. The Hopi tell of the Four Worlds, each ending in a different form of catastrophe: fire, ice, flood, and "earth changes." Each destruction, they said, was both an ending and a cleansing — a necessary turning of the spiral.

These stories may differ in detail, but they converge on the same truth: the Earth moves through cycles, and humanity moves with her.

Modern science often treats these stories as superstition, yet geological records tell a different story. We see layers of catastrophe etched into stone: abrupt climate swings, volcanic winters, magnetic field collapses, crustal shifts, and sudden extinctions. The Younger Dryas event around 12,800 years ago shows evidence of global upheaval — massive floods, wildfires, and a sudden temperature crash that reshaped the world. Recent discoveries at Göbekli Tepe hint that its builders may have been survivors of such a cataclysm, intentionally burying their temple complex to preserve it for a future age.

Sacred sites themselves may have been part of these warnings. Many structures encode astronomical cycles, particularly precession — the slow wobble of the Earth's axis over approximately 26,000 years. This cycle affects the rising and setting of constellations, marking the passage of great ages. Why did so many ancient people track precession? Because it signals larger shifts — magnetic changes, climate changes, and cosmic alignments that influence Earth's stability.

The Sphinx, with its water erosion marks, hints at an age older than the desert around it — a time when Egypt was lush, wet, and later transformed by sudden desiccation. Mayan codices track solar cycles and long-count calendars that mark not the end of the world, but the turning of an age. Andean legends speak of Viracocha, a bearded teacher who arrived after the last great flood, guiding survivors in rebuilding civilization. These are not isolated myths. They are fragments of a global memory.

The ancients were not trying to frighten future generations. They were trying to prepare them.

Knowledge was encoded into temples, calendar stones, megalithic structures, and symbolic myths so that when the next great cycle approached, humanity would recognize the signs. Some cultures placed their warnings in architecture. Others embedded them in stories. Some used astronomical alignments, while others relied on oral tradition. Different methods, one intention: remembrance.

Sacred sites aligned with solstices, equinoxes, and specific star clusters may have functioned as cosmic clocks — giant calendars marking the turning of ages, revealing when humanity approached another threshold. When certain constellations rise in particular positions, when the Earth's magnetic field weakens, when the solar cycles intensify, ancient texts say the world enters a period of great change. Not destruction for its own sake, but transition.

The elders of many Indigenous cultures still speak of such cycles today. They do not describe them as linear events, but as spirals — repeating, yet ascending. Each age offers lessons. Each collapse clears what cannot continue. Each beginning emerges from the ending of what came before. These cycles are not punishments but recalibrations. Realignments with cosmic rhythm.

Perhaps the most important message from the ancients is this: humanity has survived these cycles before. We carry the memory in our myths, our bones, and our intuition. This is why so many feel a stirring now — a sense that something is shifting, that we are approaching another threshold. It is not fear. It is recognition.

When we stand before ancient sites built with astonishing precision, we are not only seeing monuments of the past. We are seeing messages meant for the future — for us. They were placed where they are, aligned as they are, designed as they are, so that one day, when the cycle turned again, those who were ready would remember.

> Remember the patterns.
> Remember the warnings.
> Remember the resilience.

Remember the way back to harmony with the Earth.

We are not the first civilization to face great change. But we may be the first with the technology, knowledge, and consciousness to understand the full scope of these cycles and choose a different response.

The warnings of the ancients were not meant to evoke fear. They were meant to inspire preparation, awareness, and alignment. They call us to wakefulness, to presence, to remembering the larger story in which we live.

The Earth is shifting again. And the stones — still aligned, still humming, still watching — remind us that change is not an ending. It is a turning of the spiral. A doorway into the next world.

CHAPTER EIGHT — Gateways and Guardians

Some places feel different the moment you step into them. The air changes. The temperature shifts. The sound drops away or grows sharper. Your body reacts before your mind understands why. These are threshold places — gateways where the boundary between seen and unseen grows thin. Ancient cultures understood these spaces intimately. They built temples, stone circles, and ceremonial paths not to create the gateway, but to mark it.

A gateway is not a door. It is a field — a shift in the texture of reality. The land itself signals, "Here, the worlds meet." At these locations, time can stretch or pause. Thoughts grow quiet. Intuition rises. A subtle pressure surrounds you, as if you have stepped into a deeper layer of Earth's consciousness.

Guardians often accompany these gateways — not as winged figures or mythical beings, but as presences woven into the land. Some appear as ancestral memory. Some as elemental intelligence. Some as imprints of those who tended the site long ago. Their purpose is not to frighten or restrict, but to maintain the integrity of the space.

In your body, you feel them as watchfulness.

Not intimidating. Not threatening. More like stepping into someone's home — a moment of recognition that you are entering a place with its own rules, its own energy, and its own history.

These guardians exist across cultures. The ancient Egyptians spoke of threshold keepers who presided over sacred gateways, ensuring only those with the right intention could enter. The Celts believed in mound guardians who protected passage graves and stone circles. Indigenous traditions speak of spirits woven into the land — beings who watch over mountains, rivers, and ceremonial sites. In Japan, torii gates mark transitions from ordinary space into sacred space, and spirits called kami dwell within natural features. Different languages, same truth: some places are alive.

Your own experiences reflect this.

During an investigation at Gettysburg, you felt an immediate shift the moment you approached the bridge. The pressure around you changed. A boundary. A presence. A sense that you had crossed into something that was not meant to be disturbed lightly. When you stepped off the bridge, the feeling vanished. When you stepped back on, it returned. That was not imagination. That was a guardian field — an energetic threshold protecting memory, trauma, and sacred ground.

Many people feel threshold effects without realizing what they are encountering. A sudden heaviness in the chest when walking near an ancient burial site. A quiet sense of awe when stepping into a stone circle. Goosebumps near old battlefields, mountains, or temples. A subtle pushback when trying to enter a place you're not meant to enter. The land communicates, and the guardians amplify that message.

Fragmented pieces of this understanding remain in our language: "the veil is thin," "this place has a presence," "the air feels different here." These aren't poetic metaphors. They are accurate descriptions of what the body senses when stepping into a gateway.

Many sacred sites were designed intentionally to mark and stabilize these transitional zones. Passage tombs like Newgrange guide the seeker from darkness into light, mirroring the inner journey of awakening. Stone circles like Callanish and Avebury encircle energetic nodes where the Earth's grid lines cross, creating resonance pockets. Labyrinths invite you to walk in spirals that mimic the movement of consciousness returning to its center.

Even natural gateways carry this power — caves, springs, ravines, mountain passes, ancient forests. Places where Earth's magnetic field shifts or concentrates. Places where the air feels charged. Places where the land speaks.

Guardians tend these spaces not as individuals but as fields of intelligence. Sometimes they appear to sensitive people as shadows, figures, flickers of movement, or shapes that resemble animals or ancestors. More often, they are simply felt — a presence behind you, beside you, or in the air, watching without judgment.

These guardians are not here to dominate. They are here to maintain balance.

They ensure that only those who come with open intention, respect, and alignment may cross the threshold. They guide those who need guidance, nudge away those who are not ready, and hold the energetic stability of the site itself. The Earth allows many to pass through her gateways, but she does not open lightly for those who would misuse her power.

In this way, every threshold becomes a mirror.

If you approach with reverence, the space opens. If you approach with confusion or fear, the space becomes quiet, neutral, or gentle. If you approach with harmful intent, the space closes — subtly, firmly, unmistakably. You feel a sense of "not today," or a sudden unease, or a barrier of invisible pressure pushing you back.

The ancients honored these spaces with ritual because they understood that walking through a gateway requires presence. Ceremony wasn't superstition — it was alignment. A way to enter the space with clarity and respect. A way to communicate intention.

As modern seekers, we still feel these thresholds, even if we lack the language to name them. And when we do recognize them, something awakens. We begin to understand that not all sacred spaces were created by human hands. Many were revealed — discovered, not built. Marked, not made.

These places remain active today, humming beneath forests, cities, and open fields. Some are as powerful as they were thousands of years ago. Some have quieted. Others, as Earth shifts into a new cycle, are beginning to stir again.

If you feel drawn to such places, it is not accidental. Sensitivity is a form of remembering. Intuition is a form of permission. And every gateway has a guardian — not to stop you, but to guide you when you arrive with the right heart.

For those who know how to listen, the land still speaks. For those who know how to feel, the gateways still open. And for those who arrive with reverence, the guardians still welcome them.

CHAPTER NINE — The Awakening Grid

Across the world, ancient structures align not only to the stars above but to invisible pathways beneath the Earth — a vast, energetic network connecting sacred sites, natural power points, and geological nodes. This network has been called many names: ley lines, dragon lines, songlines, spirit roads, meridians, telluric currents. Different cultures described it differently, but the understanding was the same. The Earth is alive. She breathes. She pulses. And her energy moves in patterns that shape both the land and the consciousness of those who walk upon it.

This planetary grid is not symbolic. It is measurable. Subtle variations in the Earth's magnetic field form flowing pathways that carry energy much like currents in the ocean. These currents spiral, rise, converge, and diverge, creating nodes — places where the energy is amplified. Many of the world's most powerful sacred sites sit directly on these nodes: Giza, Stonehenge, Machu Picchu, Easter Island, Uluru, Delphi, Chichen Itza, Serpent Mound, Mount Shasta. It is no coincidence that temples, oracle centers, and megalithic structures cluster along these lines.

The ancients understood this energy deeply. They placed their monuments where the Earth's pulse was strongest, using stone to stabilize, amplify, and interact with these currents. Granite, quartz, basalt, and limestone were chosen intentionally — minerals with piezoelectric properties that respond to pressure, vibration, sound, and magnetic shifts. When arranged in geometric patterns, they create resonance fields that interact with the Earth's grid. In this way, sacred sites acted as tuning instruments: enhancing intuition, influencing consciousness, and anchoring energetic stability.

But this grid is not static. It moves through cycles. It expands and contracts as the Earth shifts — magnetically, geologically, and spiritually. During times of great change, these currents awaken, strengthen, or reposition. When this happens, sensitive people feel it. They describe it as a hum beneath the skin, heightened intuition, pressure in the air, sudden emotional clarity, or an inexplicable urge to visit certain locations.

Human consciousness and the Earth's grid are intertwined. When one shifts, the other responds.

There are places where these currents run especially strong. The Hopi Indians speak of energy lines that cross the land like veins, carrying spiritual force through the body of the Earth. Australian Aboriginal peoples sing the landscape into being through songlines — energetic pathways mapped through ceremony and story. Chinese geomancy describes dragon lines, energetic currents that flow through mountains and rivers, influencing fortune, vitality, and harmony. In Celtic lands, the paths between stone circles, burial mounds, and hillforts form shimmering alignments that mirror the pulse of the land.

These traditions come from cultures that never met — yet they describe the same phenomenon.

Some researchers have proposed global grid models showing geometric patterns encircling the Earth. One of the most known is the "icosahedron-dodecahedron grid," where nodes form a planetary web of triangles and pentagons. Another is the ancient meridian alignment that appears to run through Giza, connecting it to Easter Island, Nazca, Mohenjo-Daro, Angkor Wat, and other major power centers. These models differ in detail, but they converge on one truth: the Earth is structured energetically, not randomly.

Many sacred sites act as "chakras" of the planet — major energetic organs that correspond to different aspects of consciousness. The root chakra in Mount Shasta. The heart chakra in Glastonbury and Shaftesbury. The solar plexus chakra in Uluru. Whether literal or symbolic, these places radiate distinct energies that people feel instinctively. They draw pilgrims not because of reputation, but because the soul recognizes something alive in those locations — something resonant.

In times of transition, these global chakras pulse more strongly.

The Earth is currently in such a transition. Her magnetic field is weakening. Solar activity is shifting. Weather patterns are destabilizing. Geomagnetic anomalies are increasing. These are not signs of destruction, but signs of movement — a recalibration of the grid, a turning of a larger cycle.

As the Earth's energy shifts, dormant nodes activate. Old lines reconnect. New pathways form. People feel drawn to move — to relocate, to travel, to stand on mountains, to walk near water, to visit ancient sites. Some feel an undeniable calling to places they have never seen. Others feel pressure to leave places that no longer support them. These sensations are not random. They are the body responding to the Earth's energetic map as it reconfigures itself.

When the grid awakens, humanity awakens with it.

This is why so many people feel a rise in intuition, vivid dreams, emotional release, or spiritual sensitivity. It's why synchronicities multiply. Why people begin searching for meaning, for alignment, for truth. The awakening is not individual. It is planetary. The Earth's consciousness is rising, and she is pulling us with her.

Ancient builders designed their monuments not only to mark the grid but to stabilize it during these cycles. Pyramids anchored energy. Stone circles regulated flow. Temples enhanced coherence. These structures were not ceremonial alone. They were functional — part of a vast planetary system meant to support humanity through times of great change.

As the new cycle unfolds, these sites are stirring again. They hum. They pulse. They call.

Not everyone hears the call, but those who do feel it unmistakably — a resonant tug in the chest, a memory rising through the body, a sense of recognition so strong it feels like returning home. This call is not to visit every sacred site, but to reconnect with the grid consciously, intuitively, spiritually — to align your inner energy with the Earth's shifting pulse.

The Earth is waking. And as she rises into her next cycle of consciousness, the grid will continue to activate, reconnect, and recalibrate. This is not a moment of fear. It is a moment of remembering — that we are not separate from the Earth, that her pulse is our pulse, that her awakening is our awakening.

> The grid is ancient.
> The grid is alive.
> And the grid is rising again.

CHAPTER TEN — Buried Memory and Living Stone

Stone remembers.

Not in the way humans recall events, but in the way the Earth holds vibration, impression, and experience. Every place, every structure, every sacred site carries the memory of what has happened there — not as words or images, but as energy. Stone absorbs intention. It records sound. It holds emotion. And the older the stone, the deeper the memory.

Ancient cultures understood this intimately. They carved stories into rock not just to preserve knowledge, but to align human consciousness with the living memory of the land. When they built temples, pyramids, and stone circles, they were embedding information into matter — encoding wisdom into forms that could survive long after language changed and civilizations vanished.

This is why many sacred sites feel alive. They are not passive ruins but archives of consciousness, storing generations of ceremony, prayer, initiation, grief, joy, sound, and intention. You can feel it when you walk among them: a pressure in the air, a soft hum beneath your feet, a sense that the place is aware of you.

Modern science is only beginning to catch up to what the ancients already knew. In laboratories, researchers have discovered that certain minerals — especially quartz, basalt, granite, and limestone — react to pressure, sound, and electromagnetic fields. They vibrate. They generate current. They store subtle information in ways we are still trying to understand. This is the foundation of the "stone tape" theory: the idea that events, emotions, or energies imprint themselves into the environment and can be sensed, felt, or triggered later.

But the ancients didn't need theories. They experienced it directly.

Newgrange in Ireland, built more than 5,000 years ago, is aligned so precisely with the winter solstice sunrise that a beam of light travels down the passage and illuminates a stone basin deep within. On that day, the chamber fills with golden light — a literal awakening of a memory encoded in architecture. The builders intended it. They designed the temple to "remember" the return of the sun. The moment the light enters is not symbolic — it is activation.

The Great Pyramid carries similar memory. The resonance within its chambers responds to specific frequencies, amplifying them and creating waves that move through the stone. Ancient rites performed there would have been recorded not in books, but in vibration — imprinted into the structure itself. Even now, people describe feeling altered when standing inside, as if something old is stirring awake.

The landscape, too, carries memory. Battlefields hum with unresolved emotion. Mountains hold ancestral stories. Caves echo with ancient ceremonies. Springs and wells are filled with legends because people sensed something sacred in them long before religion assigned meaning. The Earth remembers because she is alive. Your own experiences reflect this truth.

At Gettysburg, the energy hit you before you saw anything. A sudden heaviness. A density in the air. A presence watching. That was memory — intense, layered, unresolved — woven into the land itself. Your body recognized it immediately. Awareness doesn't require sight. It requires resonance.

When people feel drawn to certain places but repelled by others, they are responding to memory. When they feel a rush of emotion at a temple or a standing stone, they are responding to memory. When they sense a presence that feels ancient and familiar, they are responding to memory.

This is why ancient builders used stone instead of wood. Stone endures. Stone remembers. Stone holds information through cycles of destruction and rebirth, through floods, fires, and shifting eras. Even when a temple collapses, even when a stone circle erodes, the memory remains in the fragments, in the ground, in the air around it.

Many sacred sites contain layers of memory — not only spiritual memory, but geological memory. The Earth itself records her own cycles. Patterns of magnetism. Climatic shifts. Solar changes. Catastrophic events. These patterns are encoded in rock strata, crystal formations, and mineral deposits. When ancient civilizations built on certain sites, they were often responding to the land's memory — working with the energy of places shaped by ages of Earth's history.

Human memory and Earth memory are intertwined. The body carries minerals that mirror the composition of the land. Our bones hold crystalline structures similar to the stones placed in ancient temples. This is why we feel resonance in certain places

— because the memory in the stone speaks directly to the memory in us.

The ancients knew this connection and honored it. When they built temples, they were not creating monuments to worship distant gods. They were creating libraries of consciousness — places where knowledge could be preserved in matter, where the Earth itself could safeguard wisdom through long cycles of forgetting.

Now, as the world shifts again, these memories are stirring. Sacred sites hum more strongly. Intuition rises. People feel drawn to pilgrimage, to learning, to remembering. We are not accessing new knowledge; we are reawakening ancient memory buried in our own bones.

Stone is not silent. It is alive with the stories of the Earth.

And when we listen — truly listen — we begin to remember that we are part of that story, woven into the same fabric of time, consciousness, and vibration. The memories held in living stone are not separate from us. They call to us because they are ours.

The Earth remembers. And she invites us to remember with her.

CHAPTER ELEVEN — The Sound of Stone

Long before written language, sound was the first teacher. The ancients understood that vibration shapes matter, that tone alters consciousness, and that sound interacts with stone in ways both subtle and profound. They built chambers that hum, corridors that echo like instruments, and temples where a single spoken word can expand into a chorus. Sound was not a byproduct of architecture. It was the purpose.

Every ancient culture believed that creation began with sound — the spoken word, the cosmic tone, the vibration that brought form into being. Modern physics echoes this idea: everything is frequency. Everything vibrates. Matter is slowed-down sound. The universe itself hums with background resonance. We live inside a song we are only beginning to hear.

Sacred sites were built to interact with this song.

Across the world, ancient structures amplify, modulate, or distort sound in ways that defy coincidence. In Malta's Hal Saflieni Hypogeum, a human voice speaking at 110 hertz causes the entire chamber to vibrate, affecting brainwaves and producing sensations of altered time and expanded awareness. The effect is so strong that modern researchers have limited public access to protect visitors from becoming overwhelmed.

At Chavín de Huántar in Peru, labyrinthine tunnels create acoustic illusions that make the sound of conch shells and water roar like thunder, disorienting the mind and guiding initiates into trance. In Ireland's Newgrange, a simple clap or hum echoes multiple times, as if the stone itself is singing back. In the Great Pyramid, the King's Chamber possesses near-perfect acoustic resonance — tones linger unnaturally long, and certain frequencies seem to vibrate through the body rather than through the air.

These places were not designed for casual gatherings. They were built as sonic instruments — temples of vibration where sound and stone work together to shift consciousness.

When you enter such a space, you feel it immediately. The air thickens. Your body becomes the receiver. A whisper becomes a wave. Each sound seems to touch something deeper than the ear. These chambers were created for ritual, healing, initiation, and transformation. Sound was the doorway.

The builders knew that certain frequencies can calm the nervous system, open intuitive perception, or trigger emotional release. They used chanting, drumming, singing bowls, conch shells, flutes, and harmonic overtones not merely as music but as tools. They understood the relationship between vibration and the body — how sound affects water, how frequency affects the heart and brain, how resonance can synchronize thought and emotion.

This knowledge survives today in practices like sound healing, meditation, and mantra — remnants of a much older science.

But the most profound aspect of this ancient understanding is that sound interacts with stone in predictable, measurable ways. Quartz vibrates in response to pressure and tone. Granite amplifies resonance. Limestone shapes and reflects sound. When these minerals are arranged with precision, they produce acoustic effects that influence consciousness.

Many megalithic sites contain these minerals intentionally. Stone circles often hum with low-frequency resonance during dusk or dawn, especially near equinox points. Some stones vibrate in response to wind. Others respond to footsteps. There are places where simply standing in silence allows you to feel a faint pulse — a vibration rising through the stone and into your feet, spine, and mind.

These aren't anomalies. They are signatures. The ancients chose materials not for convenience but for harmony with the Earth's frequency.

Sound is a form of memory. It carries intention. When a chant is repeated in a chamber for centuries, the stone absorbs the vibration. When drums echo against temple walls, the walls remember. When a prayer is spoken at a shrine day after day, year after year, the site becomes saturated with that frequency. Over time, the place develops a presence — an energetic imprint shaped by the sounds, rituals, and emotions that occurred there.

Some call it sacred residue. Others call it acoustic memory. But whatever the name, the effect is the same: stone becomes alive with the sound of human devotion.

Modern experiments show that sound can reorganize water molecules, create geometric patterns in sand, and influence electrical fields. If sound shapes matter so easily, imagine what centuries of ritual did to the stones of ancient temples. Imagine the layers of resonance embedded in the Great Pyramid, Stonehenge, or the Oracle chamber at Delphi. These sites are not ruins. They are vibrational archives.

The relationship between sound and consciousness is not metaphorical. Chanting slows brainwaves. Low-frequency tones induce trance. Harmonics synchronize hemispheres. Drums mimic the heartbeat of the Earth. Flutes activate emotional processing. These physiological responses would have been known to initiates and priesthoods long before we developed scientific language for them.

In a world before books, sound was the library.

Temples encoded knowledge through frequency — not in symbols carved on walls alone, but in the architecture itself. The sound of the space was part of the teaching. Initiates didn't simply "hear" the lesson. They felt it through their bones, their breath, their nervous system. Knowledge was transferred vibrationally.

This is why so many people today experience powerful reactions when entering ancient sites. The memory in the stone is awakened by the resonance in the body. The chamber recognizes the visitor, and the visitor recognizes the chamber. Something aligns. Something stirs. Something returns.

Humanity is rediscovering what the ancients always knew: sound is a bridge between worlds — inner and outer, physical and spiritual, Earth and cosmos. And stone is the perfect keeper of that bridge.

When we hum inside a temple, we are joining a conversation thousands of years old. When we sit in silence among stone circles, we hear the Earth's own vibration. When we whisper into the darkness of an ancient chamber, the echo carries the voice of memory.

> Sound reveals what words cannot.
> Stone preserves what time cannot.
> Together, they awaken what we have forgotten.

CHAPTER TWELVE — Encoded in Stone

We walk through the world as though the ancient structures around us are remnants of something finished, but they are not. The stones are still speaking. The Earth is still breathing. The memory is still alive. And we are still part of it.

Everything we have explored — spirals, star maps, gateways, grids, resonance, guardians, warnings — leads to one truth: we live upon a planet that remembers. A planet that has carried humanity through cycles of awakening and forgetting. A planet that encodes wisdom not in books, but in mountains, temples, rivers, and ruins. A planet that holds the blueprint of consciousness in her very body.

We are not separate from that blueprint. We are woven into it.

The ancients built with stone because stone outlives collapse. Because stone endures fire, flood, darkness, and the long silence between ages. Because stone can carry information across thousands of years. These builders understood that the future would need reminders — markers to guide humanity back to itself when the next cycle of remembering arrived.

That cycle is now.

Many people sense it without knowing why: a rising intuition, a soft inner voice, a pull toward the past, a feeling of being called to specific places, specific knowledge, specific truths. It is not imagination. It is resonance. The grid is awakening, and as it does, so do the memories stored within us.

We are beginning to remember what the ancients knew — that consciousness is not confined to the mind, that the Earth is a living being, and that we are connected to her through energy, rhythm, and intention. The stones remind us of this. They hold the echo of ceremony, the vibration of sound, the geometry of the stars, and the memory of cycles long forgotten.

When you stand at a sacred site, you are not only looking at history. You are standing in a conversation that crosses time. The builders knew who would come after them. They knew consciousness would fall into forgetting and rise again. They encoded their wisdom into stone so that when the world shifted once more, those who returned would feel the memory awaken inside them.

This is why ancient sites feel familiar to so many. Why the sight of old temples brings tears. Why stone circles feel like home. Why the hum of a chamber feels like a message. These places recognize you. They remember your soul, even if your mind has forgotten.

The memory is not external. It is internal.

The same minerals found in sacred stones live in your bones. The same spiral that shapes galaxies shapes your DNA. The same frequencies that move through temples move through your nervous system. You are not an observer of the ancient world. You are a continuation of it. A living expression of its wisdom returning.

The knowledge encoded in stone was never meant to stay outside you. It was meant to awaken what was already within.

We arrive at sacred places seeking answers, yearning for connection, searching for meaning — only to discover that the stones were placed not to teach us something new, but to remind us of what we already carry. They are mirrors of memory, invitations to resonance, thresholds to deeper truth.

You have felt this. Something in you recognizes the call.

The Earth is not simply awakening. She is calling her own back to remembrance — those who feel, those who listen, those who sense the subtle shifts in energy, time, and intuition. The gateways open for those who arrive not with fear or doubt, but with presence, reverence, and willingness.

In this cycle of remembering, the stones no longer serve as external teachers. They serve as catalysts — activating the memory encoded in your body, your intuition, your consciousness. The wisdom of ancient builders is not separate from your own inner knowing. It is the same wisdom, carried through time in two different forms: stone and soul.

This book ends here, but the remembering does not.

As you continue into your own life — your own awakening, your own spiral — you will find that the world begins to look different. You will notice patterns in the land, symmetry in the stars, resonance in your breath. You will sense gateways in ordinary places. You will feel the hum of the Earth beneath your feet. You will recognize the presence of guardians in places that call to you. And you will understand, without needing proof, that the sacred was never lost.

It was waiting.

Waiting for those who could feel the memory rise within themselves. Waiting for those who would listen to the stone. Waiting for those who would remember their place in the larger design.

Because what was encoded in stone was always meant to awaken what was encoded in you.

The memory lives on. The grid is alive. The spiral continues.

And you — a being of Earth and star, body and soul, matter and memory — are part of the unfolding story.

The stones have spoken. Now you remember.

CHAPTER THIRTEEN — The Stone Within

For all the journeys we take across the world — to temples, pyramids, stone circles, sacred mountains, rivers thick with legend — the greatest journey is always inward. Every megalith, every resonance chamber, every gateway, every encoded alignment ultimately leads us back to the one place all sacred paths converge: the inner temple.

The ancients understood this. They built monuments not only to mark powerful places on the Earth, but to mirror the structure of the human spirit. Outer temples were reflections of inner ones. Stone sanctuaries were reminders of the sanctuary within. Their geometry was not only cosmic; it was anatomical. Their alignments were not only stellar; they were energetic, mapping the meridians of the human body and the pathways of consciousness.

We are not simply observers of sacred architecture. We are participants. We are reflections of it.

The pyramids rise in tiered layers, just as human awareness rises through levels of understanding. Stone circles represent the cycles of life, death, rebirth, and the spiraling journey of the soul. Passage tombs lead from darkness into light, mirroring the inner journey of revelation. Caves and chambers echo the womb — the place where transformation begins. Every structure is a mirror: of the cosmos, of the Earth, and of the human spirit.

When we stand at these sites, we are meant to feel something awaken within us — the recognition that what is encoded in stone is also encoded in our bones.

Your body holds minerals found in ancient temples. Your cells carry vibrational memory. Your DNA spirals like galaxies. You are a living sacred site — walking, breathing, remembering. The same patterns that shape pyramids and standing stones shape your consciousness. The same resonance that moves through megaliths moves through your heart, your breath, your intuition.

This is why sacred places feel familiar. You are made of the same material they are.

The ancients did not separate spirituality from the body. They understood that awakening was a full-spectrum experience —

physical, emotional, energetic, and cosmic. They built temples as tools for transformation, not as destinations. The purpose was not the stone itself, but what the stone awakened in the visitor.

And so it is with you.

Your life experiences, your awakenings, your moments of resonance and recognition — these are the chambers of your inner temple. When you feel pulled toward certain places, when intuition rises, when synchronicity becomes unmistakable, you are stepping into your own sacred architecture.

The Earth calls you not to teach you something new, but to help you remember what you already carry.

For some, that remembering begins with dreams. For others, with intuition, or an inexplicable feeling of déjà vu. Sometimes it is the first time you lay your hand on an ancient stone, and something vibrates in your chest. Sometimes it is a quiet moment in nature where the world suddenly feels alive. Sometimes it comes through grief, or healing, or a turning point that cracks the old self open.

The inner temple is activated in countless ways, but the result is the same: a rising sense that life is not random. That you are connected to something vast and intelligent. That you are here with purpose, memory, and lineage — even if you cannot name it yet.

The stones remind you not because they hold the answers, but because they hold the resonance that matches your soul.

Everything you have read in this book — the spirals, the star maps, the gateways, the grid, the guardians, the sound, the memory — is not separate from you. It is not external. It is the language your soul already speaks. The architecture of your inner world.

The ancients built temples so humanity would have mirrors — reflections of what we carry inside.

Now, as the Earth moves into a new cycle, the outer mirrors and the inner mirrors converge. The sacred sites awaken as human consciousness awakens. The energy grid rises as intuition rises. The memory in the stone stirs as the memory in the body stirs.

Your awakening is part of the Earth's awakening. Your remembering is part of the cycle. Your inner temple is part of the planetary grid.

You are not visiting sacred sites. You are meeting yourself.

What the stones carry, you carry. What the Earth remembers, you remember. What is encoded in stone is encoded in you.

The next steps in your journey — whether toward new places, new insights, or new awakenings — will not arise from seeking something outside yourself. They will come from recognizing what has always been within. The purpose of the ancient world was never to teach you something you didn't know — only to help you remember what your soul never forgot.

The stone within you is awakening. The temple within you is opening. And the journey continues — not outward, but inward, where all sacred paths truly lead.

CHAPTER FOURTEEN — The Conversation Continues

The journey through ancient stone is not something that ends when you close this book. If anything, this is where the real journey begins. The remembering awakened in you now will continue to unfold in subtle ways — in intuition, in synchronicity, in dreams, in the way certain landscapes feel familiar or alive. You may find yourself looking at the world differently, noticing patterns you overlooked before, sensing the presence of something deeper beneath the ordinary.

This shift is not accidental. It is resonance. When consciousness touches truth, it expands.

You may begin to feel drawn to certain places without knowing why. You may wake with images of stone chambers, spiral pathways, or ancient stars that feel strangely like memory. You may sense gateways in places you've passed a hundred times. You may find yourself remembering things you never learned — knowing without knowing how you know.

This is what happens when inner and outer worlds begin to align. The Earth's wisdom awakens your own.

The ancients understood that knowledge does not arrive all at once. It comes in layers, spirals, thresholds, cycles. It unfolds in the way sunrise reaches a valley — slowly, softly, then all at once. They built their temples as teachers, not as final destinations. They knew that each person's awakening would be unique, triggered by different experiences, different moments, different initiations.

Perhaps the greatest initiation is simply learning to listen.

Not with the ears, but with the body. Not with the mind, but with the field of awareness that surrounds you. The stones taught through vibration. The temples taught through echo. The Earth teaches through intuition, sensation, stillness, and subtle knowing. When you begin to feel these teachings, you are participating in the same lineage of consciousness that shaped the ancient world.

This journey is not about becoming someone new. It is about remembering who you have always been.

You are not an outsider studying the ancient mysteries. You are part of the continuum — a soul returning in a new cycle of remembering. The wisdom of the ancients is not separate from your own inner intelligence. Their knowledge was encoded for you, carried through time for those who would awaken now.

If you feel called to explore deeper, follow that call gently. Let intuition guide you, not urgency. The Earth reveals herself to those who approach with reverence, curiosity, and humility. There will be moments of clarity, moments of confusion, moments where you feel the hum of truth without having the words for it. Trust that. Trust yourself.

The path of remembering is not linear. It spirals.

You will return to ideas with new eyes. You will revisit memories with new understanding. You will feel the Earth differently as your resonance changes. You may even find that certain places feel like home in a way you cannot explain — echoes of past lifetimes, ancestral threads, or soul agreements rising to the surface.

The journey continues not through more seeking, but through deepening presence.

The world around you is alive with messages, patterns, synchronicities, and quiet invitations to awareness. When you walk outside, notice how the land feels. Notice the places that draw you or push you away. Notice where your breath deepens, where your thoughts quiet, where your inner vision sharpens. These are your personal sacred sites. Your gateways. Your teachers.

The stones spoke to you in these chapters, but they were never speaking alone. They were awakening the stone within — the part of you that remembers your origin, your path, your connection to Earth and cosmos. The conversation continues now not in words, but in resonance.

As you move forward, trust the unfolding.

Trust the guidance rising from within.

Trust the subtle signs the world places along your path.

You are part of a living story — ancient, ongoing, and rising into a new cycle. The remembering that began in these pages will continue to echo through your intuition, your experiences, and the temple of your own inner knowing.

The stones have spoken. The Earth has answered. Now the conversation is yours to continue.

CHAPTER FIFTEEN — Memory In The Landscape: The Earth as an Active Participant

The Earth is not a static backdrop to human history. It is an active, shifting system that records its own changes over vast spans of time. Geological layers, climate cycles, volcanic ash deposits, fossil soils, shoreline remnants, and magnetic signatures capture information so reliably that scientists can reconstruct events that occurred thousands or millions of years before written records existed. This long-term environmental memory provides the context within which human societies developed, adapted, and built. Stone architecture survives because it interacts with this memory rather than resisting it. Understanding ancient structures requires understanding the Earth that shaped them.

Geology preserves evidence of dramatic events that influenced human settlement patterns. Volcanic layers provide time markers that appear across continents. Ash deposits from major eruptions—some local, some global—form thin, identifiable bands in sediment cores and archaeological sites. These layers reveal when landscapes were altered, when communities were displaced, and when climates shifted abruptly. Earthquakes leave their own signatures in fault scarps, uplifted coastlines, and disrupted sediment layers. Over time, these geological traces accumulate into a clear record of the pressures that ancient people faced. Human societies responded to these events through migration, rebuilding, or adaptation. The Earth's memory captures the environmental causes even when cultural explanations have disappeared.

Climate archives contain equally detailed records. Ice cores extracted from Greenland and Antarctica document temperature fluctuations, atmospheric composition, solar activity, and volcanic eruptions across hundreds of thousands of years. Tree rings reveal drought cycles, rainfall variability, and ecological stress. Lake sediments and peat bogs preserve pollen, charcoal, and microfossils that reflect long-term environmental change. These natural archives show that climate variability—not stability—has been the norm throughout human history. Periods of rapid cooling, warming, or shifting rainfall patterns often align with archaeological evidence of settlement change. When societies moved, consolidated, or abandoned regions, their decisions were shaped by forces recorded in these environmental layers.

Landscape alteration created by humans also becomes part of the geological record. Terracing, irrigation canals, quarry sites, ancient roads, and cleared fields modify soil structure in ways that persist long after communities have vanished. These traces reveal the scale of human effort devoted to adapting the environment for farming, building, or ceremony. In some cases, the landscape retains evidence of repeated use over centuries, showing how knowledge was passed forward through generations. In other cases, abandoned systems mark periods of decline or relocation. The Earth preserves both the signs of human creativity and the marks of human absence.

Soil chemistry and micro-remains offer additional clues. Burn layers reflect the use of fire for land clearing or domestic purposes. Phytoliths—tiny silica structures left behind by plants—survive where other organic materials decay, revealing which crops were grown or gathered. Animal bones and isotopic signatures indicate diet, mobility, and domestication practices. These micro-level details contribute to a broader understanding of how people interacted with their environments. They show the continuity of subsistence strategies, the impact of climate on agriculture, and the shifts in resource use that occur when ecosystems change.

The Earth also preserves evidence of forces that operate beyond human control. Changes in sea level following the last Ice Age reshaped coastlines rapidly compared to the pace of cultural memory. Entire settlements were inundated as shorelines retreated inland. Many ancient communities likely experienced these changes gradually within a few generations—slow enough to avoid catastrophic collapse but fast enough to require adaptation. Today, their former locations lie underwater, preserved only through marine archaeology and geological reconstruction. These submerged landscapes illustrate how environmental memory extends far beyond what stone architecture alone can show.

Modern observation provides a valuable parallel to ancient experience. Tracking volcanic activity, seismic clusters, solar variability, atmospheric anomalies, and oceanic shifts offers insight into the same types of environmental pressures that shaped human history. While the timescales differ, the underlying processes remain constant. The Earth continues to evolve, and contemporary monitoring reveals patterns that geological records show have occurred repeatedly throughout the past. Observing these changes today—whether through scientific instruments or diligent personal tracking—mirrors the attentiveness of ancient peoples who watched the sky, the seasons, and the land for signs of change.

Ancient societies likely responded to environmental fluctuations with the same blend of awareness, adaptation, and uncertainty that modern observers experience. They noticed shifts in weather patterns, animal behavior, water availability, and celestial cycles because their survival depended on it. Over generations, these observations became part of cultural knowledge systems. Structures aligned to solar or seasonal markers reflect this long-term attentiveness. Agricultural strategies, settlement choices, and ritual practices emerged from the need to interpret and respond to environmental rhythms. In this sense, human memory and Earth memory intersect: one is short and cultural; the other is long and geological.

Earth memory places ancient structures into a broader temporal framework. A stone circle that marks a solstice is part of a climate pattern extending beyond human lives. A terraced hillside reflects agricultural adaptation to long-term rainfall variability. A settlement abandoned due to drought corresponds to changes preserved in pollen records. Stone architecture is not simply a human artifact; it is a material response to environmental forces recorded across deep time. When we interpret these structures through this lens, they become part of an ongoing dialogue between people and planet.

Recognizing the Earth as an active participant in human history does not diminish the achievements of ancient societies. Instead, it highlights their resilience and ingenuity. They built within constraints, adapted to cycles, and responded to long-term environmental shifts with creativity and persistence. The landscapes they inhabited retain evidence of these choices even when cultural memory has faded. By reading Earth memory alongside the archaeological record, we gain a clearer understanding of the conditions that shaped human development. The stones that survive reflect not only human skill but also the enduring influence of the planet itself.

CHAPTER SIXTEEN — The Continuity of Human Ingenuity

Human societies have always been shaped by the need to adapt to their environment, solve practical problems, and create structures that support communal life. Across thousands of years, people in different regions developed unique architectural traditions, symbolic languages, and methods of understanding the world. Despite this diversity, a consistent theme emerges from the archaeological record: ingenuity is a defining characteristic of the human story. Stone structures from different eras and regions demonstrate how communities used available resources, responded to environmental challenges, and built forms of continuity that extended beyond individual lifespans. This ingenuity did not arise from extraordinary origins or hidden knowledge. It reflects the capacity of ordinary people to experiment, observe, and refine solutions over generations.

Innovation emerges wherever people face similar needs. The development of shelters, storage systems, ceremonial spaces, and defensive structures occurred independently in multiple regions. These inventions do not reflect shared origins but shared circumstances. For example, elevated platforms appear in various cultures because they serve practical functions: protection from flooding, improved visibility, or the creation of communal gathering spaces. Stone alignments appear in different parts of the world because tracking the sun's movement is essential for agriculture. Monumental enclosures arise where communities gather seasonally. The recurrence of certain architectural forms demonstrates parallel problem-solving rather than long-lost global connections. The ingenuity lies in the ability to adapt general principles to specific landscapes.

Adaptation has been central to human survival. Climate fluctuations, resource changes, and environmental pressures forced communities to adjust their practices. In some regions, societies responded to drought by developing irrigation systems or shifting agricultural strategies. In others, they relocated settlements or diversified subsistence methods. Architectural changes often reflect these shifts. Structures were rebuilt, repurposed, or abandoned as conditions evolved. Terraces, canals, and storage facilities reveal long-term responses to environmental variability. Stone buildings expanded or contracted depending on population shifts. These adaptive strategies underscore the flexibility of human societies and the enduring relevance of local knowledge.

Cultural continuity depends on intergenerational learning. Skills related to quarrying, carving, construction, and orientation were transmitted through apprenticeship and repeated practice. This long-term accumulation of knowledge explains the complexity of ancient architecture more effectively than theories of lost civilizations or sudden leaps in capability. Each generation contributed incremental refinement. A community that built simple enclosures in one century might construct more elaborate monuments in the next. The continuity of practice, rather than any singular moment of innovation, accounts for the evolution of architectural traditions. Stone structures thus represent not only physical durability but also the persistence of cultural knowledge across time.

The ingenuity reflected in ancient architecture is not limited to monumental projects. Small-scale innovations—domestic design, storage solutions, water management, and community organization—demonstrate a consistent pattern of practical creativity. Houses built close together reflect social cooperation and shared resource networks. Local materials shaped construction methods and aesthetic choices. Decorative carvings and symbolic patterns reveal cognitive and artistic complexity. The combination of practical design and expressive detail shows how early societies integrated function with meaning. These everyday innovations are often overlooked in favor of monumental structures, yet they reveal the depth of human problem-solving in daily life.

Ingenuity persists even when cultural traditions change. When populations moved into new regions, they adapted older practices to new conditions. When societies encountered environmental stress, they applied inherited knowledge to revised circumstances. When communities absorbed influences from trade or migration, they integrated new ideas into existing systems. This continuity across change demonstrates that human creativity is resilient and iterative. Cultural shifts do not erase earlier knowledge; they transform it. The archaeological record reveals how these transformations unfold across centuries and how resilience underlies cultural evolution.

The stones that survive—temples, terraces, plazas, enclosures, dwellings, and sculptures—represent only a small portion of the thousands of innovations that shaped ancient life. Most human ingenuity was expressed through perishable materials or practices that leave no trace. Social cooperation, oral knowledge, ecological understanding, and everyday craftsmanship shaped communities as strongly as monumental architecture. The surviving stone structures are the visible edge of a much broader creative landscape. They endure because they are durable, not because they are the only examples of human innovation. Recognizing this helps avoid overstating the significance of monumental sites while acknowledging the skill and creativity present across all levels of society.

Understanding the continuity of ingenuity clarifies the broader message of the archaeological record. Human societies did not progress along a simple upward trajectory. They adapted, expanded, contracted, reorganized, and reinvented themselves in response to countless pressures. Their achievements were cumulative, collaborative, and grounded in observation and experimentation. The structures they left behind demonstrate the capacity for long-term planning, social coordination, and creative expression. They reflect the persistence of human memory—both cultural and structural—across generations.

The ingenuity found in ancient stone architecture connects the earliest builders to people today. The desire to understand the environment, create stability, mark meaning, and build for the future remains constant. Modern technologies change the tools available, but the underlying impulses remain the same. Across thousands of years, the continuity of human creativity is evident in every stone placed with intention. What survives in the landscape is a testament to this enduring capacity—proof that ingenuity is not confined to any particular era but woven into the fabric of human life.

CONCLUSION — What The Stones Remember

Stone endures because it binds human intention to the long memory of the Earth. While most materials of daily life fade within years or centuries, stone carries traces of human activity across deep time. The structures that remain—temples, circles, terraces, corridors, dwellings—represent the portion of ancient life that could withstand erosion, climate shifts, and the continual reworking of landscapes. They do not tell the whole story of early societies, but they preserve enough to reveal how people adapted, organized, created, and interpreted their world. The stones that survive are not mysterious relics; they are fragments of human resilience.

This book has followed a path from the largest scale to the smallest—from Earth cycles and geological memory, to global architectural patterns, to individual sites, to carvings made by single hands. Each chapter has shown that the archaeological record is neither chaotic nor encrypted. It is shaped by natural processes, available materials, and the accumulated choices of countless individuals. The people who built with stone did so for practical, social, and symbolic reasons. Their accomplishments reflect long-term observation, generational learning, cooperative labor, and a deep engagement with the landscapes they inhabited.

The gaps in our knowledge do not suggest lost civilizations or forgotten technologies. They reflect preservation bias, environmental decay, and the absence of written records for much of human history. Most ancient societies built primarily with materials that do not survive. What remains is extraordinary precisely because it is rare. The absence of evidence outside these stone structures is not evidence of erased cultures—it is the natural result of time acting on fragile materials. Recognizing this helps distinguish between the limits of archaeology and the allure of myth.

Myths themselves are meaningful, not because they provide literal history but because they express how cultures interpreted their environment. Stories of floods, lost lands, or vanished societies reflect real experiences reframed through narrative. They preserve emotional truth rather than empirical fact. When examined alongside geology and archaeology, myths offer insight into how people responded to environmental change. But they cannot be used as direct evidence for historical events. Understanding their symbolic nature allows us to appreciate their richness without distorting the material record.

Scientific tools illuminate what the stones can confirm and what remains beyond reach. Dating methods, material analysis, remote sensing, and experimental reconstruction reveal how structures were built, when they were modified, and how they relate to broader environmental patterns. These methods do not answer every question, but they provide a stable foundation for interpreting what survives. The most responsible approach to ancient architecture avoids overreaching claims and instead focuses on evidence that can be measured, repeated, and verified.

The stones also reveal the continuity of human creativity. The same problem-solving instincts appear across regions and eras. Different societies developed similar architectural forms because they faced similar challenges, not because they shared a forgotten ancestor. Each community built according to its environment, needs, and accumulated knowledge. These local solutions created global patterns that reflect the universality of human ingenuity. Innovation did not require extraordinary origins; it arose from ordinary people working together over long periods of time.

Modern observation of Earth systems provides a valuable perspective on ancient life. The cycles of climate, tectonic activity, solar variability, and environmental change that shape the world today also shaped the lives of early builders. The pressures recorded in geological archives mirror the disruptions that communities navigated thousands of years ago. Their responses—migration, adaptation, construction, ritual, and memory—demonstrate a continuity between past and present. By reading the Earth's long memory alongside surviving structures, we gain a clearer understanding of how human societies endured shifting conditions.

What the stones remember is not a hidden world or a forgotten origin but the story of humanity itself. They reveal cooperation, persistence, and the ability to create meaning within an uncertain environment. They show how people sought stability in the face of change, how they recorded the rhythms of the sky and the land, and how they built structures that outlasted their own lives. The stones remind us that human history is not defined by sudden leaps or vanished ages but by continuous adaptation and enduring creativity.

In the end, the memory encoded in stone is a testament to the ordinary brilliance of early societies. It reflects the accumulated insight of generations who observed their world carefully and responded with craftsmanship, organization, and intention. The structures they left behind allow us to witness a small part of their experience. They are fragments, but they are enough. Through them, we see a human story shaped not by mystery, but by ingenuity—and preserved not by chance, but by the enduring memory of the Earth itself.

Epilogue — The Memory We Carry Forward

The stones that survive across the world remind us that memory takes many forms. The Earth remembers through layers of rock, ash, and sediment. Human cultures remember through structures, stories, and traditions. And individuals remember through intuition, experience, and the quiet sense that we are connected to something larger than ourselves.

The archaeological record reveals how early societies responded to the challenges of their environment with creativity and resilience. Yet no amount of stone can capture the full depth of human life—the hopes, fears, beliefs, and meanings that shaped the people who built these structures. Much of what they felt and understood exists now only in faint traces or in the intuition of those who sense a thread of continuity stretching back through time.

As I wrote this book, I often found myself reflecting on the ways in which physical memory and inner memory coexist. The Earth holds the evidence of cycles and upheavals that shaped ancient societies. The human spirit holds its own form of continuity—an internal awareness that reaches across generations. Neither form of memory is complete on its own, but together they reveal a larger truth: that we are part of a long, unfolding story shaped by both the world around us and the world within us.

This book is not the end of that exploration. It is the part that grounds the larger series—the reminder that our spiritual and intuitive experiences exist within a physical context shaped by deep time. The stones tell us where we have been. The soul tells us why it matters.

What we carry forward is both.

Also by Rooted Hound Press

Rose Pocket Sanctuary Series

The Rose Codex
Mary Magdalene: A Sanctuary of Remembrance
The Magdalene Path

Books by Rooted Hound Press

Returning to Wholeness: An Invitation to the Soul
Echoes Through the Spiral: A Soul's Continuum
Healing the Past Through the Present
Let It Find Me Ready
Encoded in Stone: The Memory of Earth & the Story of Us

Journals & Companions

Floral Journal
Celestial Journal
Rooted Hound Journal: A space for reflection and renewal
(Additional themed journals coming soon)

Published by Rooted Hound Press
Vienna, New Jersey
www.rootedhoundpress.com